Investigate

Mapping

Louise Spilsbury

Heinemann Library
Chicago, Illinois

Edited by Siân Smith, Rebecca Rissman, and Charlotte Guillain
Designed by Joanna Hinton-Malivoire
Original illustrations © Capstone Global Library
Picture research by Elizabeth Alexander and Sally Cole
Originated by Modern Age Repro House Ltd
Printed and bound in China by Leo Paper Group

14 13 12 11 10
10 9 8 7 6 5 4 3 2 1

Library of Congress Cataloging-in-Publication Data

Spilsbury, Louise.
  Mapping / Louise Spilsbury.
     p. cm. – (Investigate geography)
  Includes bibliographical references and index.
  ISBN 978-1-4329-3473-6 (hc) – ISBN 978-1-4329-3481-1 (pb) 1.
Maps–Juvenile literature. I. Title.
  GA105.6.S75 2009
  912–dc22
                                        2009011047

www.heinemannraintree.com
Visit our website to find out more information about Heinemann-Raintree books.

To order:

☎ Phone 888-454-2279

🖥 Visit www.heinemannraintree.com to browse our catalog and order online.

Acknowledgments
The author and publishers are grateful to the following for permission to reproduce copyright material: Alamy pp. **4** (© Itani Images), **21** (© Betty LaRue), **23** (© Dennis MacDonald), **29** (© Gorilla Photo Agency Ltd); Getty Images pp. **6** (Dan Callister), **20 & 30 bottom right** (Victoria Blackie); iStockphoto p. **25** (© Freeze Frame Studio); Photolibrary pp. **5** (Wave RF), **7** (Thomas Frey/imagebroker.net), **9** (Comstock/Creatas), **10** (Gonzalo Azumendi/Age Fotostock), **14** (Steve Vidler/Imagestate), **15** (Nicolas Thibaut/Photononstop), **19** (Mike Berceanu), **22** (Mike Tittel/OSF).

Cover photograph of a map of Europe on a globe reproduced with permission of Alamy/© Brownstock Inc.

Every effort has been made to contact copyright holders of material reproduced in this book. Any omissions will be rectified in subsequent printings if notice is given to the publishers.

Contents

Some words are shown in bold, **like this.** You can find out what they mean by looking in the glossary.

What Are Maps?

A map is a drawing of a part of the world. There are many kinds of maps. Some maps show things like streets and buildings or hills and mountains. They help us find our way around. Weather maps show us what the weather will be like.

➡ Some maps have pictures of the real-life objects we want to find.

Maps of the countryside help to stop people from getting lost.

Most maps show only things that are there all the time, like hills and houses. Maps of places do not usually show things like cars or people. Some maps, such as weather maps, show something that moves or changes.

Making Maps

Maps are often made from **aerial** photographs. People take aerial photographs from an airplane or **satellite** that flies or hovers above Earth. Aerial photographs show what Earth looks like from above. Aerial photographs then decides what needs to be on the map.

What does a map of this school need to show?

CLUES

- Where is the field?
- Which parts of a school are always there?

A map of a school needs to show the buildings and places that are there all the time. These are the school's **permanent** features.

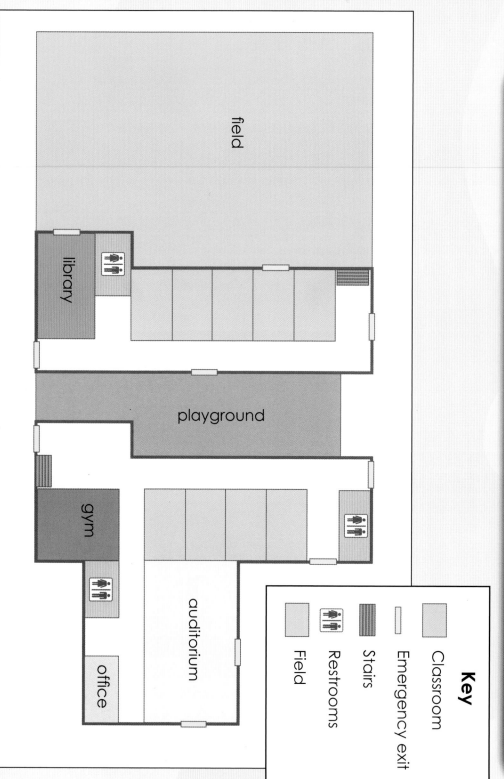

field

library

playground

gym

auditorium

office

Key

Classroom

Emergency exit

Stairs

Restrooms

Field

This map shows where the buildings, restrooms, and office are. It shows pathways. The **labels** help to explain where things are.

Maps show:

➤ **aerial** views of a place

➤ where things are

➤ connections between places, such as paths or roads

➤ important features

Street Maps

Cities have many buildings and roads, rail and subway lines, and buses. Cities have **services** that people need like hospitals, post offices, and schools. They also have play areas like parks, swimming pools, and sports centers.

Street maps show the many features found in a town or city.

How can you find the hospital on this street map?

Key
- Bike path
- Post office
- Library
- Hospital
- Fire station
- Police station
- School
- Town hall
- Downtown
- Parking

Oak Avenue
Main Street
Brook Avenue
Willow Road
Elm Avenue
New Road
Cedar Avenue
Everett Avenue

CLUES

- Some features on maps are shown by letters instead of **labels.**

- If P stands for Parking, what letter might be used for a hospital?

You can find out how the hospital is shown on the map by looking at the **key**. The hospital is marked by the letter H. It can be found on the map between Elm Avenue and New Road.

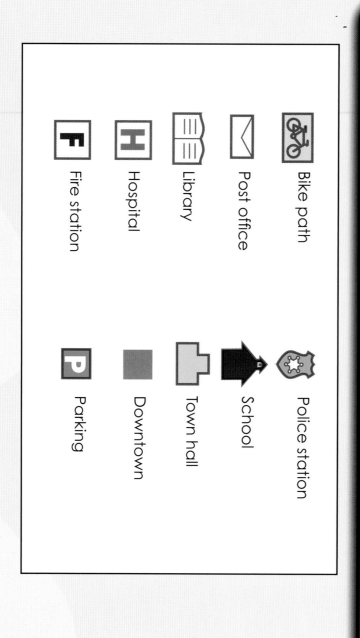

Bike path

Police station

Post office

School

Library

Town hall

Hospital

Downtown

Fire station

Parking

Mapmakers save space by using **symbols** like this to show different features. The symbols can be pictures, shapes, or letters. A map key tells us what the symbols mean.

Transportation maps help people find their way around a big, busy city. They show connections between places. This map shows the stops on a subway route. The different routes are in different colors.

The distances between places on a transportation map are not always as they would be in an **aerial** photo. Some distances are longer, some are shorter.

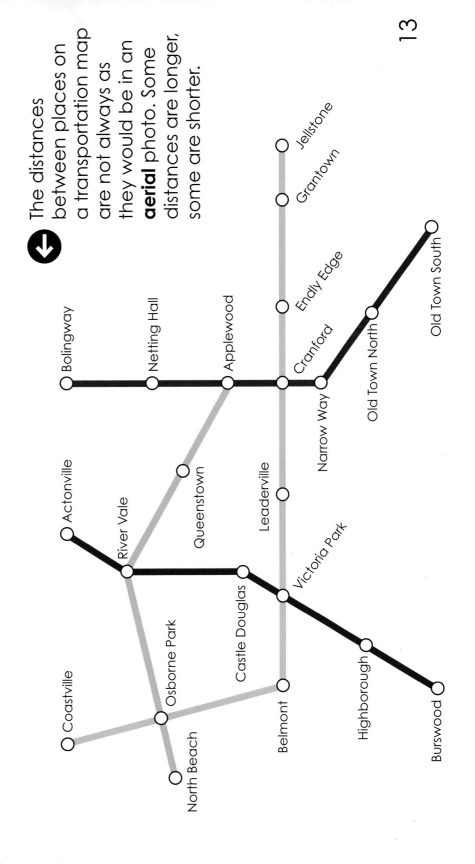

Mapping the Land

There are few roads in the countryside. Land maps have to show natural features that are in the country, like hills and mountains, woods, rivers, lakes, and fields.

Q How are rivers shown on maps?

CLUE
- What color are rivers?
- What does a river look like from above?

Most maps show rivers as a blue line.

On this map, the blue line of the river shows that it flows into a lake. The road crosses the river over Eagle Bridge. The woods are shown by areas of green with little tree **symbols**.

Key

Lake
River
Woods
House
Bridge

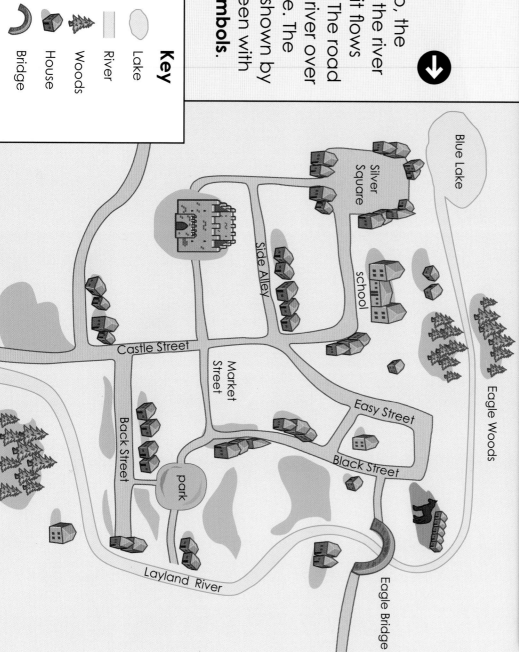

Blue Lake

Silver Square

school

Eagle Woods

Side Alley

Castle Street

Market Street

Easy Street

Black Street

Back Street

park

Layland River

Eagle Bridge

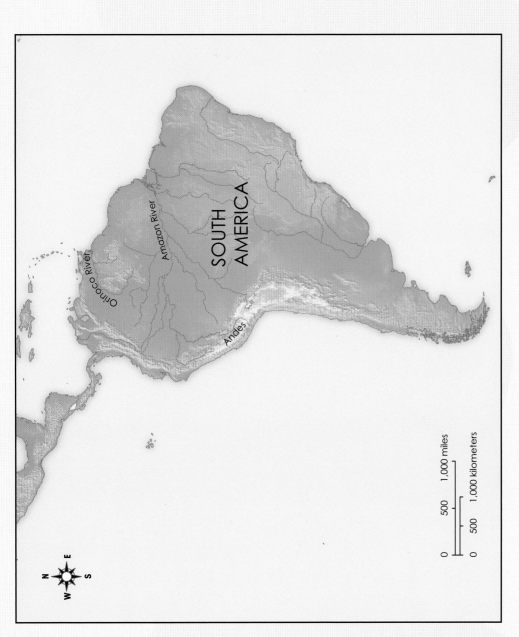

North
West East
South

Orinoco River

Amazon River

SOUTH
AMERICA

Andes

0   500   1,000 miles

0   500   1,000 kilometers

Physical maps use different colors to show different
kinds of land. On this map of South America, the blue
lines are rivers. The blue patches are lakes. High hills
and mountains are yellow and white.

World Maps

This is a map of the world. It shows the **continents** and oceans. Continents are the seven largest **landmasses** in the world. Some flat world maps show different features. They may show mountain ranges or capital cities.

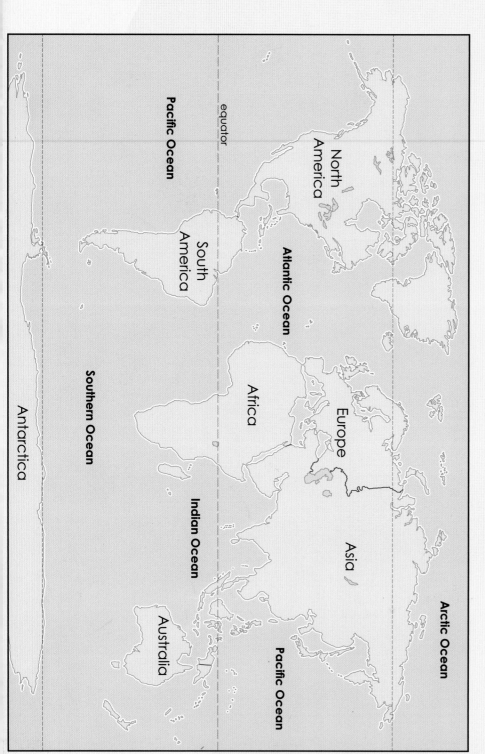

North America

South America

Pacific Ocean

equator

Atlantic Ocean

Africa

Europe

Asia

Arctic Ocean

Indian Ocean

Pacific Ocean

Australia

Southern Ocean

Antarctica

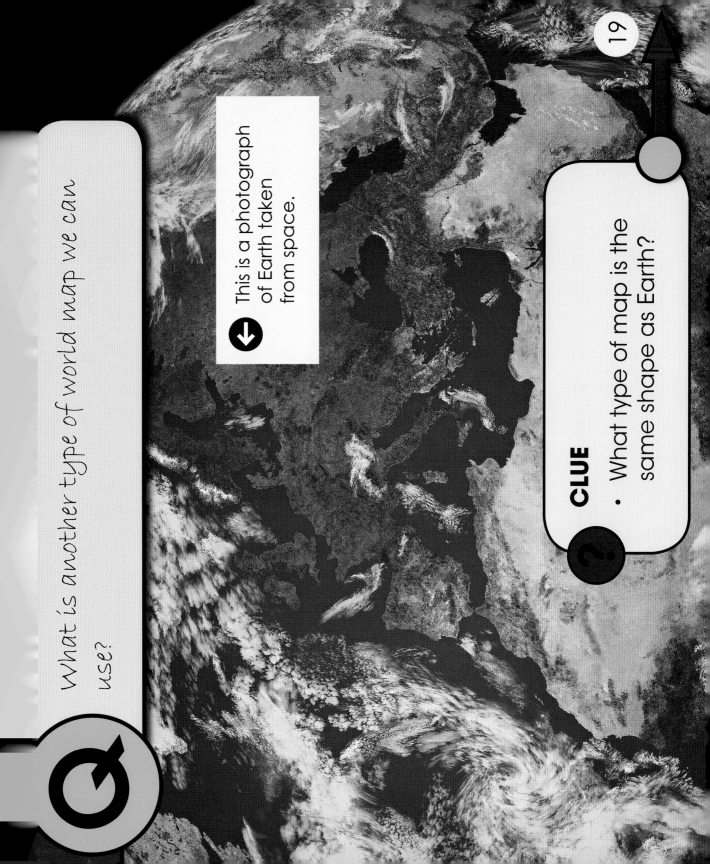

Q What is another type of world map we can use?

This is a photograph of Earth taken from space.

CLUE

? · What type of map is the same shape as Earth?

A

We can also use a globe. A globe is a round, ball-like model with a map of Earth on it.

Globes are the most accurate type of maps of Earth. They show Earth as round, just as it is in real life.

The North Pole is at the top of the globe. The South Pole is at the opposite end. The Poles are the coldest places on Earth.

North Pole

South Pole

equator

The equator is an imaginary line around the middle of a globe. It marks the halfway point between the North and South Poles.

Using Maps

To use a map, there are three other things you need to know:

- how to use **compass** points
- how to use a **grid**
- how to figure out **scale**.

The needle of a compass always points north. People use a compass to find directions.

How do compass points help us use a map?

CLUE

- What can you find on many maps other than a **key**?

Many maps have a **compass symbol** or a **directional arrow**. This helps you to read directions on the map.

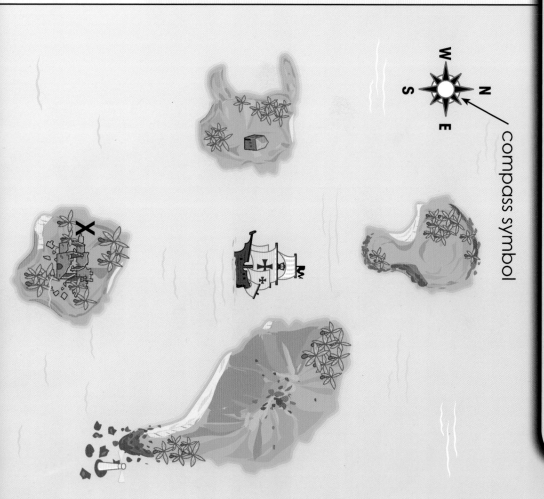

compass symbol

You can use north, east, south, and west to follow directions on a map. On this treasure map, the treasure is hidden on the island to the south, just west of the ruins!

The four directions, north, south, east, and west, do not describe every direction. To give a direction somewhere in between you can say, for example, "northwest" or "southwest."

TIP

You can remember compass directions with a sentence like "Never Eat Slimy Worms." It reminds us of the names of each compass point as you go clockwise around the compass.

Many maps have sets of lines that form **grid** squares. A **grid reference** is the letters or numbers that meet at each square. A grid reference helps us find a place on a map.

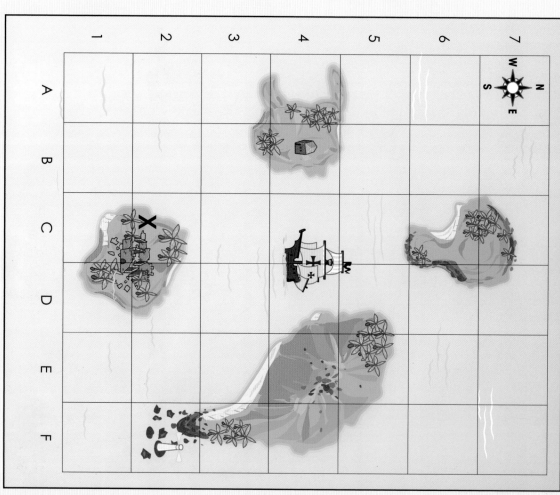

This treasure map grid has letters going across (horizontally) and numbers going up (vertically). The grid reference for the lighthouse is F, 2 and the hut is B, 4.

This map has numbers along both sets of grid lines. Grid references for this map are made of four numbers. To find a grid reference, first look at the numbers along the bottom of the map. Then go up that grid line to get the next number.

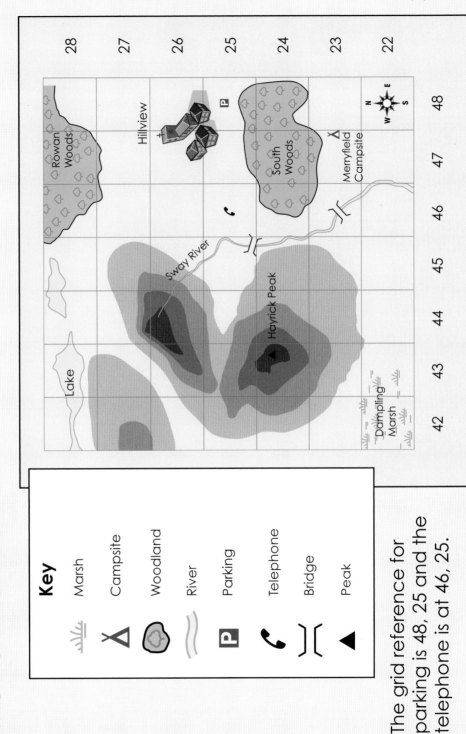

Key

❄	Marsh
⅄	Campsite
🟢	Woodland
〰	River
🅿	Parking
☎	Telephone
)(	Bridge
◀	Peak

The grid reference for parking is 48, 25 and the telephone is at 46, 25.

Different maps use different **scales**. The scale bar tells us how much smaller a feature is on the map than it is in real life. For example, a scale of 1 inch: 2 miles means that 1 inch on the map equals 2 miles on the ground.

On this map, the distance between Wild Rock and Underwood is about 10 miles.

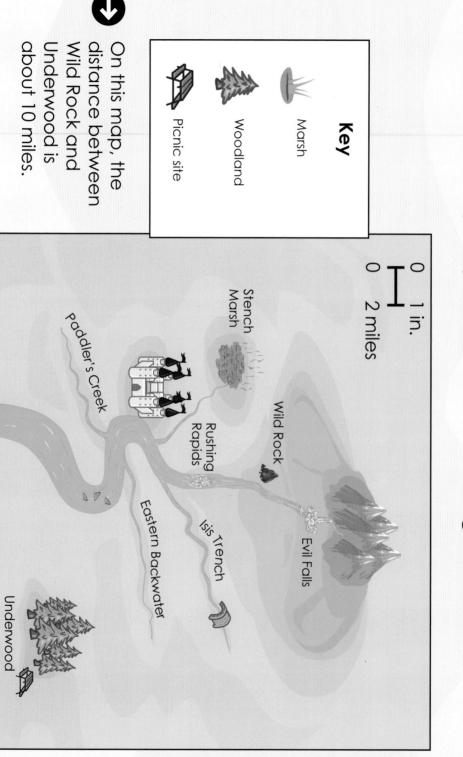

Key

Marsh

Woodland

Picnic site

0   1 in.

0   2 miles

Stench Marsh

Paddler's Creek

Rushing Rapids

Wild Rock

Eastern Backwater

Isis Trench

Evil Falls

Underwood

Maps are useful for telling us where a place is. Today, more and more people use **GPS** systems instead. These electronic gadgets use **satellites** to find your location and guide you to where you want to go. They can show maps on a screen that change as you move.

This GPS system speaks to drivers to tell them which direction to take. The arrow on the map also shows drivers where they need to go.

Checklist

Maps are drawings of places. We use maps to find where things are. There are different kinds of maps, such as:

land maps

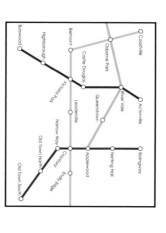

transportation maps

plan maps

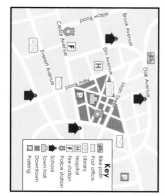

street maps

world maps

Glossary

aerial overhead, from the sky

compass object with a needle that always points north. People use compasses to help them find directions.

continent one of the seven largest landmasses in the world

directional arrow arrow on a map that shows one of the directions north, south, east, and west. Some directional arrows are drawn to look like a real compass.

GPS short for "Global Positioning System." A GPS system gets information from satellites to tell you its exact location on Earth.

grid pattern of lines on a map

grid reference numbers or letters that tell you the location of something on a map that has a grid

key list of words or phrases that explain symbols on a map

label short description that identifies something for a reader

landmass large continuous area of land

permanent something that is always there

satellite object in space that sends out TV signals or takes photographs

scale difference between the size of something in real life and its size on a map

service job or business that supplies people in a settlement with something they need, such as electricity or water

symbol pictures, shapes, or letters that represent objects in real life

Index